Introduction

Freelance Flourish: Navigating the Gig Economy with Confidence

A BOOK BY
MAHDI HASAN

Copyright Information

Table of Contents

Chapter 1: The Freelancer's Frontier

Welcome to the Gig Economy

In today's rapidly evolving world, traditional notions of work and employment are being reshaped by the rise of freelancing. The gig economy, characterized by short-term contracts and freelance work, has opened up new horizons for individuals seeking flexibility, autonomy, and the opportunity to harness their unique skills. This chapter serves as your gateway to understanding the landscape of freelancing and what it means to be a part of the gig economy.

The Rise of Freelancing

Gone are the days when the standard career path meant a nine-to-five job in a corporate office. Freelancing, once considered an alternative choice, has now become a legitimate career option embraced by millions around the world. The advent of digital platforms, the democratization of technology, and the increasing demand for specialized services have paved the way for freelancers to take center stage. From graphic designers and writers to programmers and consultants, freelancers represent a diverse community of professionals contributing their talents to a global marketplace.

Pros and Cons of Freelancing

Like any career choice, freelancing comes with its own set of advantages and challenges. The allure of setting your own schedule, choosing your projects, and working from anywhere is undeniably appealing. On the flip side, the irregular income, lack of job security, and responsibility of managing all aspects of your business can be daunting. This chapter will help you weigh the pros and cons, enabling you to make an informed decision about whether freelancing aligns with your goals and lifestyle.

Setting the Stage: Is Freelancing Right for You?

Before diving headfirst into the world of freelancing, it's essential to take a moment of introspection. Ask yourself: Are you prepared for the independence that freelancing offers? Can you handle the uncertainty that comes with an ever-changing workload? Are you motivated enough to manage your time effectively and consistently deliver high-quality work? This chapter will guide you through self-assessment exercises designed to determine if freelancing is a suitable path for your aspirations and circumstances.

Chapter 2: Navigating the Landscape

Finding Your Niche

In the vast landscape of freelancing, finding your niche is like discovering your own patch of fertile ground in a diverse field. Your niche is the intersection of your skills, passion, and market demand. It's where your expertise shines brightest and where clients seek your unique offerings. This section will guide you through the process of identifying your niche, understanding its potential, and positioning yourself as an expert within it.

Identifying Market Demand

Freelancing is not just about doing what you love—it's about meeting the needs of clients who value your expertise. To succeed, you must identify the areas where there's a genuine demand for your services. Research industry trends, study competitors, and engage with your target audience to gain insights into what solutions they're seeking. By aligning your skills with market demand, you increase your chances of attracting clients who are willing to invest in your offerings.

Competing in a Crowded Marketplace

In a digital world where anyone can hang up a virtual shingle, standing out is crucial. Your ability to differentiate yourself from the competition will determine your success as a freelancer. From your branding and messaging to your unique selling proposition (USP), every element plays a role in carving out your space in the marketplace. Learn how to effectively communicate your value and establish a compelling online presence that captures the attention of potential clients.

Crafting Your Freelance Brand

Your brand is more than just a logo—it's the essence of who you are as a freelancer. It's the promise you make to your clients and the experience you deliver. Crafting a strong freelance brand involves understanding your target audience, defining your core values, and consistently portraying your brand personality across all touchpoints. This section delves into the art of creating a brand that resonates with clients and sets you apart as a trusted professional.

Chapter 3: Building Your Freelance Toolkit

Essential Tools for Freelancers

In the dynamic world of freelancing, the right tools can make all the difference in your efficiency and professionalism. From communication and project management to invoicing and collaboration, this section covers a range of essential tools that can streamline your workflow and enhance your freelance journey. Discover the must-have software, apps, and platforms that can elevate your freelancing game.

Creating a Professional Online Presence

Your online presence is your virtual storefront, and it's often the first impression potential clients have of you. Crafting a professional online presence involves more than just setting up a website—it's about curating a digital portfolio that showcases your work, communicates your expertise, and builds trust with your audience. Learn how to create a compelling online portfolio and optimize your website for maximum impact.

Harnessing the Power of Social Media

Social media is more than just a platform for sharing cat videos—it's a powerful tool for freelancers to connect with clients, showcase their work, and build a community. This section explores strategies for leveraging platforms like LinkedIn, Instagram, and Twitter to network, engage, and attract clients. From crafting engaging content to building a meaningful online brand, discover how to harness the potential of social media for your freelance career.

Developing a Portfolio That Shines

Your portfolio is your visual resume, a collection of your best work that demonstrates your skills and expertise. A well-structured and visually appealing portfolio can leave a lasting impression on potential clients. This section provides tips on curating an effective portfolio, selecting the right pieces to showcase, and presenting your work in a way that highlights your strengths. Whether you're a designer, writer, or developer, learn how to create a portfolio that shines.

Chapter 4: Finding Your First Gigs

The Art of Freelance Job Hunting

Securing your first freelance gigs can be both exciting and challenging. This section equips you with strategies and techniques to effectively navigate the job-hunting process. From searching job boards to networking with potential clients, learn how to cast a wide net and identify opportunities that align with your skills and interests.

Freelance Platforms and Marketplaces

Freelance platforms and marketplaces are virtual marketplaces where clients and freelancers connect for project collaboration. This section explores popular platforms such as Upwork, Fiverr, and Freelancer, providing insights into how to create a winning profile, craft compelling proposals, and stand out in a competitive landscape. Discover the dos and don'ts of leveraging these platforms to kick-start your freelancing journey.

Networking for Freelancers

Networking is a cornerstone of freelancing success. Building relationships with fellow freelancers, industry professionals, and potential clients can lead to valuable opportunities. Learn how to navigate networking events, online communities, and social gatherings to expand your circle, share experiences, and uncover potential collaborations. This section also delves into the art of effective communication and relationship-building.

Pitching Your Services Effectively

Crafting a persuasive pitch is an essential skill for freelancers. Whether you're reaching out to potential clients via email, attending networking events, or participating in freelancing forums, your ability to convey your value proposition concisely can make or break your chances of landing gigs. This section provides insights into tailoring your pitches, showcasing your expertise, and building a portfolio of successful pitches.

Chapter 5: Navigating Client Relationships

The Freelancer-Client Dynamic

Client relationships are the cornerstone of a successful freelancing career. This section explores the dynamics of freelancer-client interactions, emphasizing the importance of clear communication, trust-building, and mutual understanding. Learn how to establish a strong foundation for client relationships that can lead to repeat business and positive referrals.

Effective Communication and Expectation Setting

Effective communication is the linchpin of successful projects. From project scope and timelines to expectations and deliverables, this section guides you through the art of setting clear communication channels and ensuring that both you and your clients are on the same page. Discover strategies for managing feedback, addressing concerns, and maintaining open lines of communication throughout the project lifecycle.

Setting Rates and Negotiating Contracts

Determining your rates and negotiating contracts can be challenging for freelancers. This section provides insights into pricing strategies, understanding the value of your services, and navigating negotiations with confidence. Whether you're setting hourly rates or project-based fees, learn how to strike a balance between competitive pricing and fair compensation for your skills.

Handling Difficult Clients and Disputes

Even the most skilled freelancers encounter difficult clients and project disputes. This section equips you with strategies to handle challenging situations professionally and effectively. From managing client expectations to addressing disagreements and handling project revisions, learn how to navigate potential pitfalls and turn challenges into opportunities for growth.

Chapter 6: Managing Your Freelance Business

Balancing Time and Tasks

Time management is a critical skill for freelancers who juggle multiple projects, deadlines, and responsibilities. This section provides strategies for creating effective schedules, prioritizing tasks, and maintaining a healthy work-life balance. Learn how to harness productivity techniques and tools that allow you to stay organized and maximize your efficiency.

Financial Management and Budgeting

Managing your finances is essential for maintaining stability and growth in your freelance business. From tracking income and expenses to creating a budget that aligns with your financial goals, this section offers practical insights into managing your money effectively. Discover how to set aside taxes, plan for irregular income, and create a financial safety net for unforeseen circumstances.

Tax Considerations for Freelancers

Navigating the world of taxes as a freelancer can be complex, but understanding your tax obligations is crucial. This section sheds light on tax considerations, including how to classify your income, deductions you may be eligible for, and how to stay compliant with tax laws. Learn how to keep accurate records, work with accountants or tax professionals, and ensure that tax season doesn't catch you off guard.

Health Insurance and Benefits

Freelancers often lack the benefits offered by traditional employment, such as health insurance and retirement plans. This section explores options for obtaining health coverage, retirement planning, and creating a safety net for unforeseen health-related expenses. Discover resources and strategies to safeguard your well-being and financial security as a freelancer.

Chapter 7: Elevating Your Freelance Game

Scaling Up: Hiring Subcontractors and Teams

As your freelance business grows, you may find yourself with more work than you can handle alone. This section explores the option of scaling up by hiring subcontractors or assembling a team. Learn how to delegate tasks, maintain quality control, and effectively manage a group of freelancers who contribute to the success of your projects.

Diversifying Income Streams

Relying solely on a single source of income can leave you vulnerable to market fluctuations. Diversifying your income streams can provide stability and open up new opportunities. This section delves into ways to expand your revenue sources, whether through offering complementary services, creating digital products, or exploring passive income avenues.

Building Long-Term Client Relationships

While landing new clients is exciting, nurturing long-term relationships is equally important. This section explores strategies for turning one-time projects into ongoing collaborations. Discover how to exceed client expectations, offer value-added services, and become a trusted partner that clients turn to for all their future needs.

Leveraging Testimonials and Referrals

Testimonials and referrals serve as powerful tools to attract new clients and establish credibility. This section provides guidance on requesting and showcasing client testimonials, as well as strategies for encouraging referrals from satisfied clients. Learn how to harness the positive feedback from your work to build a strong reputation in the freelance community.

Chapter 8: Embracing Continuous Growth

The Importance of Skill Enhancement

In the ever-evolving landscape of freelancing, staying relevant requires a commitment to continuous learning and skill enhancement. This section explores the value of upskilling, reskilling, and expanding your skill set to meet changing client demands. Discover resources, courses, and strategies to stay ahead of the curve and provide exceptional value to your clients.

Staying Relevant in a Rapidly Changing Landscape

Technology and industry trends can reshape the freelance landscape overnight. This section discusses the significance of staying informed about market shifts and emerging technologies. Learn how to adapt your skills, services, and strategies to remain competitive in a dynamic environment, ensuring that you remain a sought-after professional in your field.

Overcoming Freelancer Burnout

The flexibility of freelancing comes with its own challenges, including the risk of burnout due to long hours, tight deadlines, and the absence of traditional workplace boundaries. This section offers strategies to recognize and prevent burnout, from effective time management to setting boundaries and practicing self-care. Discover how to maintain your well-being while pursuing your freelance aspirations.

Balancing Freelancing and Personal Life

Achieving a healthy work-life balance is essential for long-term success as a freelancer. This section explores techniques for setting boundaries, managing your time effectively, and maintaining a fulfilling personal life. Learn how to avoid the trap of constantly being "on" and find harmony between your professional and personal pursuits.

Chapter 9: Showcasing Success

Case Studies of Successful Freelancers

Learning from the experiences of others is a valuable way to glean insights and inspiration. This section presents case studies of successful freelancers who have navigated challenges and achieved remarkable milestones in their careers. Discover their strategies, lessons learned, and the pivotal moments that propelled them to success.

Success Stories from Various Niches

Freelancing spans a multitude of industries and niches, each with its unique set of opportunities and challenges. This section showcases success stories from freelancers in diverse fields, from writing and design to programming and consulting. Gain a deeper understanding of how freelancers have carved out their own paths to success and how their journeys can inform your own.

Lessons Learned and Tips from Accomplished Freelancers

Behind every successful freelancer are lessons learned from trial and error, experiences that have shaped their growth. This section offers a collection of practical tips and wisdom shared by accomplished freelancers. Whether it's advice on client relationships, financial management, or self-care, these insights can serve as guiding principles for freelancers at any stage of their journey.

Inspiring the Next Generation of Freelancers

The world of freelancing thrives on innovation and fresh perspectives. This section explores how seasoned freelancers can contribute to the growth of the freelance community by mentoring and inspiring newcomers. Learn about initiatives, resources, and platforms that empower aspiring freelancers to step confidently into the gig economy and create their own success stories.

Chapter 10: Looking Ahead

The Future of Freelancing

As the gig economy continues to evolve, so too does the landscape of freelancing. This section explores trends, technologies, and shifts that are shaping the future of freelance work. From the rise of remote collaboration to the impact of automation and artificial intelligence, gain insights into what lies ahead and how freelancers can position themselves for success in the years to come.

Predicting Trends and Innovations

Anticipating trends and staying ahead of industry innovations is essential for freelancers to remain competitive. This section delves into the process of trend analysis and provides examples of emerging trends in various fields. Discover strategies for adapting to change, embracing innovation, and leveraging new opportunities to propel your freelance career forward.

Preparing for Market Shifts

The freelance landscape is susceptible to market shifts influenced by economic, technological, and societal changes. This section explores strategies for preparing for and weathering market shifts. Learn how to diversify your skills, expand your service offerings, and remain agile in response to changing client demands. Gain insights into how adaptability can be a freelancer's most valuable asset.

Embracing Change and Staying Adaptable

In a world of constant change, adaptability is the key to survival and success. This section offers a final message of encouragement and guidance for freelancers to embrace change with an open mindset. Learn how to cultivate resilience, seek continuous learning, and approach challenges as opportunities for growth. Remember that as the freelance landscape evolves, so too does your capacity to thrive within it.

Chapter 11: The Art of Marketing and Self-Promotion

Creating a Strong Personal Brand

In the competitive world of freelancing, a strong personal brand is your beacon of identity. This section explores the elements that contribute to a memorable brand, from your unique value proposition to your visual identity. Learn how to define your brand's personality, values, and mission, and discover strategies to effectively communicate your brand across all touchpoints.

Utilizing Content Marketing to Attract Clients

Content marketing is a powerful tool for demonstrating your expertise, building trust, and attracting clients. This section delves into content creation strategies, from blogging and video content to social media posts and ebooks. Learn how to craft valuable content that addresses your target audience's pain points, establishes your authority, and positions you as a go-to resource in your field.

Leveraging Networking Events for Growth

Networking is more than just handing out business cards—it's about building meaningful relationships that can lead to collaborations and referrals. This section provides guidance on attending industry events, online networking platforms, and community engagement. Discover how to make lasting connections, share your expertise, and leverage networking opportunities to expand your freelance network.

Optimizing Online Presence for Client Attraction

Your online presence serves as a virtual storefront for potential clients. This section explores strategies for optimizing your website, social media profiles, and online portfolio to attract and engage clients. Learn how to use search engine optimization (SEO) techniques, showcase your work effectively, and create a user-friendly experience that encourages visitors to become clients.

Chapter 12: The Power of Negotiation and Contracts

Navigating the Art of Negotiation

Negotiation is a skill that can significantly impact your freelance business's success. This section delves into the principles of effective negotiation, from understanding client needs to advocating for fair compensation. Learn how to strike a balance between your value as a professional and the client's budget, and discover techniques for building win-win agreements that set the stage for successful collaborations.

Creating Comprehensive Contracts

Contracts are the foundation of a strong freelancer-client relationship. This section provides insights into creating clear and comprehensive contracts that outline project scope, timelines, payment terms, and expectations. Learn how to safeguard your interests by addressing potential scenarios, such as scope creep, revisions, and deadlines. Discover the essential components of a contract that protect both parties and foster trust.

Handling Disputes and Managing Client Expectations

Disagreements and misunderstandings can arise in any working relationship. This section offers strategies for addressing disputes in a professional and constructive manner. Learn how to manage client expectations from the outset, communicate effectively to avoid misunderstandings, and navigate disagreements with diplomacy. Discover how resolving conflicts can actually strengthen your relationship with clients.

Ethics and Transparency in Freelance Negotiation

Maintaining ethical conduct during negotiation is paramount for building trust and credibility. This section explores ethical considerations in negotiations, including honesty, transparency, and delivering on promises. Learn how to advocate for your value while adhering to ethical standards, and understand when to walk away from opportunities that do not align with your principles.

Chapter 13: Maximizing Productivity as a Freelancer

Unlocking Time Management Techniques

Time is a precious resource for freelancers, and effective time management is essential for success. This section explores a variety of time management techniques, from the Pomodoro Technique to the Eisenhower Matrix. Learn how to prioritize tasks, allocate time efficiently, and create a daily schedule that optimizes your productivity while allowing for breaks and personal time.

Tools for Task Organization and Project Management

Freelancers wear many hats, often managing multiple projects simultaneously. This section introduces tools and platforms that can help you stay organized and on top of your tasks. Explore project management software, task tracking apps, and collaboration tools that streamline communication with clients and help you meet deadlines without feeling overwhelmed.

Strategies for Overcoming Procrastination

Procrastination can hinder your productivity and impact the quality of your work. This section provides insights into overcoming procrastination through various techniques. Learn how to identify the root causes of procrastination, create a conducive work environment, and employ strategies such as the "Two-Minute Rule" and "Eat the Frog" method to tackle tasks head-on.

Creating Efficient Workflows

Efficient workflows are the backbone of a productive freelance career. This section guides you through the process of creating streamlined workflows that minimize unnecessary steps and maximize output. Learn how to identify bottlenecks, automate repetitive tasks, and create standard operating procedures that ensure consistency and quality in your work.

Chapter 14: Crafting Compelling Proposals and Pitches

Understanding the Art of Proposal Writing

Crafting persuasive proposals and pitches is an essential skill for freelancers to win clients and projects. This section dives into the art of proposal writing, from understanding client needs to tailoring your solutions. Learn how to structure your proposals, highlight your value proposition, and showcase your expertise in a way that resonates with potential clients.

Tailoring Pitches to Client Needs

Every client is unique, and so should be your approach in crafting pitches. This section explores the importance of customizing your pitches to address specific client needs and pain points. Discover how to research your clients, understand their goals, and present your solutions in a way that demonstrates your understanding and ability to deliver results.

Presenting Your Value Proposition

Standing out in a competitive freelance landscape requires effectively communicating your value proposition. This section provides insights into presenting your skills, experience, and track record in a compelling manner. Learn how to showcase your portfolio, share client success stories, and demonstrate why you're the ideal choice to meet your potential clients' needs.

Overcoming Common Pitching Challenges

Pitching can come with its own set of challenges, from addressing objections to handling client inquiries. This section offers strategies for overcoming common pitching hurdles and turning them into opportunities. Learn how to anticipate and address objections, handle pricing discussions, and navigate questions with confidence and professionalism.

Chapter 15: Freelance Ethics and Professionalism

Upholding Ethical Conduct

Ethics are the foundation of a reputable freelance career. This section explores the principles of ethical conduct that guide your interactions with clients, colleagues, and the broader freelance community. Learn about honesty, integrity, and transparency as you navigate client relationships, collaborations, and business decisions with an unwavering commitment to ethical standards.

Maintaining Client Confidentiality

Confidentiality is a cornerstone of professionalism in freelancing. This section emphasizes the importance of safeguarding client information and respecting non-disclosure agreements. Discover how to handle sensitive data, ensure secure communication channels, and build trust by demonstrating your dedication to protecting your clients' confidentiality.

Balancing Client Needs with Ethical Considerations

Freelancers often encounter situations that challenge their ethical stance. This section provides insights into striking a balance between client needs and ethical considerations. Learn how to address requests that conflict with your principles, communicate potential ethical concerns to clients, and explore alternative solutions that align with your values.

Contributing Positively to the Freelance Community

Ethical freelancing extends beyond individual interactions to the freelance community as a whole. This section explores ways to contribute positively to the community by sharing knowledge, providing mentorship, and fostering collaboration. Discover how you can engage in ethical business practices while also uplifting and supporting fellow freelancers in their journey.

Conclusion

Embracing Your Freelance Journey

Congratulations! You've embarked on a journey that offers endless possibilities and opportunities for growth. The world of freelancing is dynamic, challenging, and immensely rewarding. As you've navigated the pages of this book, you've gained insights into the intricacies of freelancing—from finding your niche to managing client relationships, and from maximizing productivity to upholding ethical standards.

Remember Your Value

Always remember that as a freelancer, you bring a unique set of skills, experiences, and perspectives to the table. Your contributions matter, and your expertise is valued by clients seeking solutions to their challenges. Embrace your role as a valuable professional who has the power to make a meaningful impact on projects, businesses, and industries.

Continuing the Learning Journey

While this book provides a comprehensive guide to freelancing, the journey doesn't end here. The world of freelancing is ever-evolving, and your growth as a freelancer is a continuous process. Stay curious, stay open to learning, and adapt to the changing landscape. Seek out new skills, trends, and opportunities that align with your passions and goals.

Building a Fulfilling Freelance Career

As you move forward in your freelance career, remember that success is not just measured by financial gains, but by the satisfaction of doing work you love, making a difference, and living life on your own terms. Embrace challenges as opportunities for growth, celebrate your achievements, and stay committed to delivering excellence in all that you do.

Thank you for joining me on this journey through the world of freelancing. May your freelance path be filled with creativity, innovation, and a sense of purpose that drives you to new heights. Your journey is yours to shape, and the possibilities are endless. Here's to your continued success as a freelancer!

Appendix

Resources for Freelancers

Congratulations on completing this book! As you continue your journey in the world of freelancing, consider utilizing the following resources to support your growth, enhance your skills, and stay informed:

1. Freelance Platforms and Marketplaces:
Explore platforms such as Upwork, Fiverr, Freelancer, and more to find freelance opportunities across various industries.
2. Online Courses and Learning Platforms:

Websites like Coursera, Udemy, and LinkedIn Learning offer a wide range of courses to help you upskill and expand your expertise.

3. Professional Associations and Communities:
Join freelancing communities and associations related to your field, such as the Freelancers Union, to connect with fellow freelancers, gain insights, and access valuable resources.
4. Books on Freelancing:
Continue your learning journey with books that dive deeper into specific aspects of freelancing, such as negotiation, marketing, and financial management.

5. Networking Events and Webinars:
Participate in virtual and in-person networking events, conferences, and webinars to connect with industry

professionals, potential clients, and fellow freelancers.

6. Online Tools and Apps:

Leverage productivity tools, project management software, and communication apps to streamline your work processes and enhance collaboration with clients.

7. Freelance Tax Resources:

Consult tax resources and professionals to navigate the complexities of freelance taxes, deductions, and compliance with local regulations.

8. Online Portfolios and Website Builders:

Create and showcase your portfolio using platforms like Behance,

WordPress, or Squarespace to display your work and attract potential clients.

9. Freelance Contract Templates:
Access contract templates to customize and use for your client agreements, ensuring clarity and protection for both parties.

10. Online Communities:
Engage in online communities and forums specific to your field to connect with like-minded professionals, share experiences, and seek advice.

Remember, the freelance journey is unique to each individual, and these resources are here to support you as you navigate your path to success. Continuously seek opportunities for growth, stay adaptable to change, and never stop investing in your personal and professional development.

The End

www.ingramcontent.com/pod-product-compliance
Lightning Source LLC
LaVergne TN
LVHW051748050326
832903LV00029B/2795